Pythons AND Garter Snakes

HENRY THATCHER

PowerKiDS press.

New York

Published in 2014 by The Rosen Publishing Group, Inc.
29 East 21st Street, New York, NY 10010

First Edition

Produced for Rosen by Cyan Candy, LLC
Editor: Joshua Shadowens
Designer: Erica Clendening, Cyan Candy

Photo Credits: All images www.shutterstock.com, except p. 19 by Martha de Jong-Lantink/
Wikimedia Commons.

Library of Congress Cataloging-in-Publication Data

Thatcher, Henry, author.
 Pythons and garter snakes / by Henry Thatcher. — First edition.
    pages cm. — (Big animals, small animals)
 Includes index.
 ISBN 978-1-4777-6110-6 (library) — ISBN 978-1-4777-6111-3 (pbk.) —
 ISBN 978-1-4777-6112-0 (6-pack)
 1. Pythons—Juvenile literature. 2. Garter snakes—Juvenile literature. 3. Snakes—Juvenile
 literature. I. Title.
 QL666.O67T45 2014
 597.96—dc23
                        2013022471

Manufactured in the United States of America

CPSIA Compliance Information: Batch #W14PK2: For Further Information contact Rosen Publishing, New York, New York at 1-800-237-9932

Table of Contents

Meet THE Python AND THE Garter Snake

Snakes come in many sizes, from huge pythons to the tiny Barbados threadsnake. Most snakes, such as the garter snake, are somewhere in between these two extremes. Pythons are huge and slow-moving, while garter snakes are small, slim, and fast. If these two snakes had a race, the garter snake would win. If the contest were arm wrestling, or squeezing other animals to death, the python would come out on top!

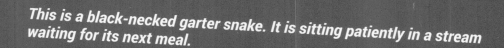

This is a black-necked garter snake. It is sitting patiently in a stream waiting for its next meal.

Garter snakes are often called garden snakes, because they are a common visitor to backyard gardens. You won't find a python in your garden, or at least let's hope not! Let's find out more about these big and small snakes.

BIG FACT!

There are around 35 species of garter snake.

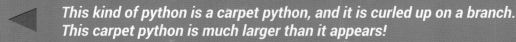

This kind of python is a carpet python, and it is curled up on a branch. This carpet python is much larger than it appears!

Where IN THE World?

Pythons live in many places around the world. They are found in Africa, south of the Sahara, in Nepal, India, Burma, southern China, Southeast Asia, Australia, and on many islands in the Philippines and Indonesia. They have been introduced into the United States, and have become an **invasive species** in Florida's Everglades. There they pose a threat to American alligators, crocodiles, and many other **native** animals. This is not good news for the Everglades ecosystem.

Here a Burmese python goes for a swim in the Everglades, in Florida. Burmese pythons are one of the largest snakes in the world.

BIG FACT!

Garter snakes are sometimes called ribbon snakes. This is likely because they are long and thin, and their stripes give them a ribbon-like appearance.

The garter snake is widespread throughout North America. It ranges from Alaska to Central America, and is found in states from coast to coast. Both kinds of snakes are sometimes kept as pets.

7

Many Different Homes

Pythons live in **tropical** places. The Burmese python lives in the jungles and marshes of Southeast Asia. Other pythons live in rain forests, grasslands, woodlands, and swamps.

The ball python lives in grasslands, savannas, and areas with a few trees in western Africa. They like to live in empty mammal burrows and termite mounds.

Water pythons live in Australia and Papua New Guinea. The live in hollow logs, along riverbanks, and in thick vegetation. Despite their name, they do not always live near water, though some do.

African rock pythons live in many habitats, including forests, savannas, semi-deserts, and rocky areas. They like to live on the edges of swamps, lakes, and rivers the best.

A Burmese python is keeping itself cool in a small pond. These snakes can grow up to 19 feet (5.74 m) long!

GARTER SNAKE

Garter snakes live in many different habitats throughout North America. They can **adapt** to life in many different **biomes**.

The common garter snake is the only species of snake to make its home in Alaska. It is also one of the northernmost species of snake in the world. Most snakes need to live in warmer places than chilly Alaska! They live in other North American states, too. They live in forests and grasslands. In the winter, they make dens in the cracks of rocks, ant mounds, or old mammal burrows. They reuse these dens each year.

The eastern garter snake likes to live near water or in wetter areas. It can be found along marshes, streams, woods, meadows, parks, gardens, weed patches, farms, and forest edges.

In this picture a small garter snake is peeking out from some leaves. You can see its small size in comparison to the leaves.

Are They Alike?

Pythons and garter snakes may be different in size, but they are both snakes. Snakes are long, have no arms or legs, and they have flexible bodies. Snakes are also ectothermic, or cold-blooded. This means their bodies are the same **temperature** as their surroundings. They must bask in the Sun to warm up or find a cool spot if they get too hot.

SLEEPING PYTHON

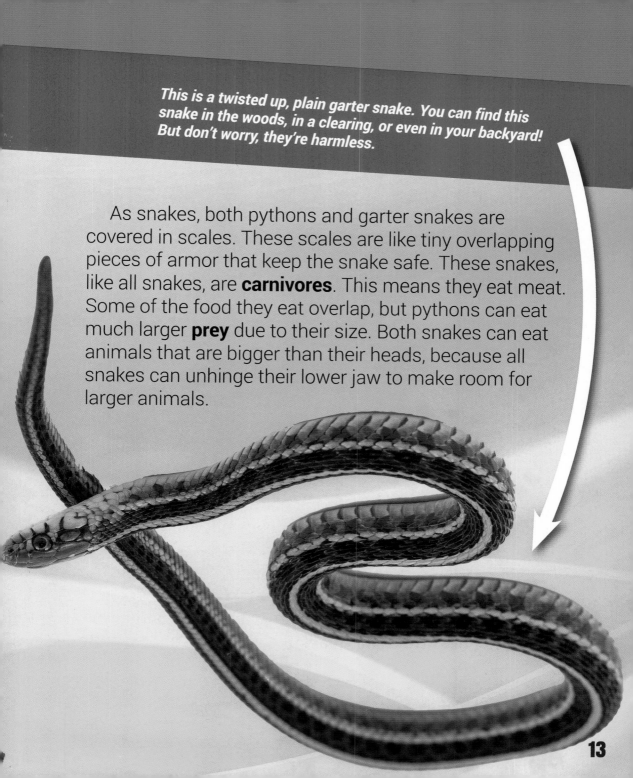

This is a twisted up, plain garter snake. You can find this snake in the woods, in a clearing, or even in your backyard! But don't worry, they're harmless.

As snakes, both pythons and garter snakes are covered in scales. These scales are like tiny overlapping pieces of armor that keep the snake safe. These snakes, like all snakes, are **carnivores**. This means they eat meat. Some of the food they eat overlap, but pythons can eat much larger **prey** due to their size. Both snakes can eat animals that are bigger than their heads, because all snakes can unhinge their lower jaw to make room for larger animals.

13

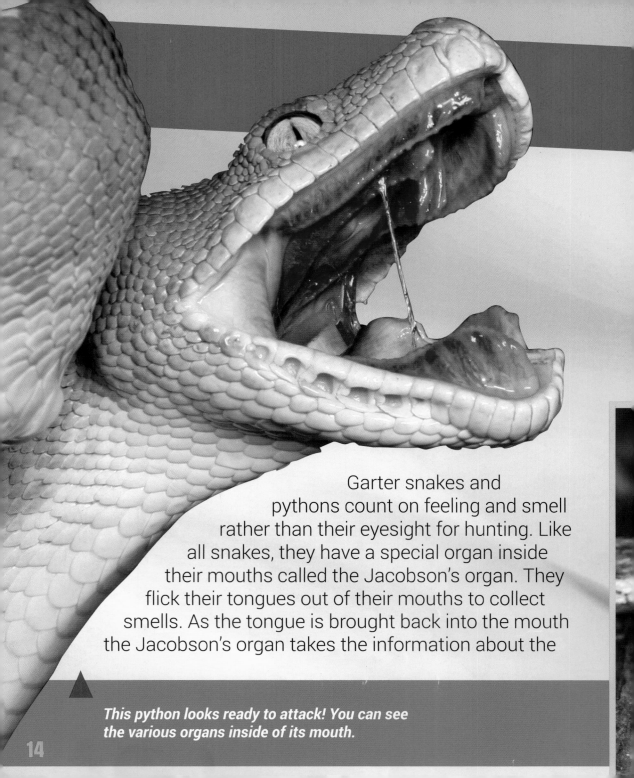

Garter snakes and
pythons count on feeling and smell
rather than their eyesight for hunting. Like
all snakes, they have a special organ inside
their mouths called the Jacobson's organ. They
flick their tongues out of their mouths to collect
smells. As the tongue is brought back into the mouth
the Jacobson's organ takes the information about the

*This python looks ready to attack! You can see
the various organs inside of its mouth.*

Here you can see the inside of a garter snake's mouth. It has similar parts to that of the python.

BIG FACT!

Before shedding starts a milky matter forms under a snake's old skin. The snake starts loosening the old skin by rubbing its nose and mouth against the ground. They then slither slowly forward leaving their old skin behind in one long piece.

smells. The snake uses the information to find prey or avoid being eaten.

Another way pythons and garter snakes, and all snakes, are alike is that they shed their skin as they grow. Young snakes shed once a month or so, but they shed less often once they are adults.

Comparing PYTHONS

Size............. 23 inches (60 cm) to 33 feet (10 m)

Habitat ....rain forests, woodlands, and swamps

Diet.............. carnivores

Predators ....big cats, hyenas, and wild dogs

Prey............rodents, lizards, birds, and mammals

Life Span.....up to 35 years

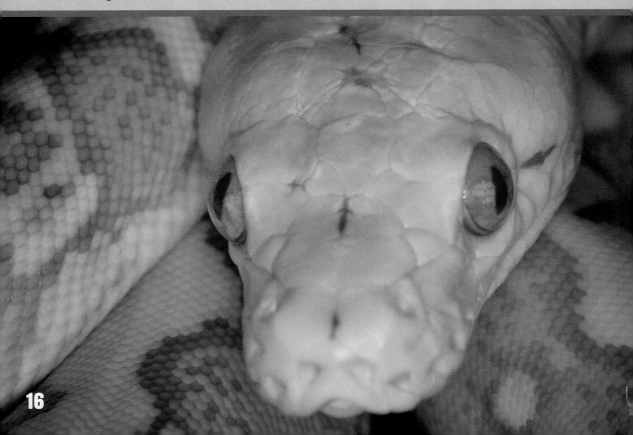

AND GARTER SNAKES

Size .... 20 to 30 inches (50–75 cm)

Habitat..... meadows, woodlands, and near water

Diet .... carnivores

Predators . hawks, raccoons, crayfish, and other snakes

Prey......... slugs, lizards, frogs, insects, and eggs

Life Span.. up to 30 years

The largest python is the reticulated python. It grows to be around 33 feet long (10 m). The smallest python is called the anthill python. It grows to be only about 2 feet (60 cm) long. Most pythons are on the larger side, though. There are 26 known species.

Pythons are constrictors. This means they do not use **venom** to kill their prey. Instead they coil their strong bodies around an animal and squeeze. The animal **suffocates**. Then the python swallows the prey whole.

BIG FACT!

You might wonder how pythons breathe while they are swallowing their prey. They have a special tube in their mouths that stays open and off to one side so they can take in air.

Pythons do not move by moving their body from side to side as some snakes do. Instead they "rib walk." They slowly move forward in a straight line by tightening the ribs and then lifting some of the scales on their belly forward. This is not a fast way to move. Pythons take about an hour to travel 1 mile (1.6 km). It takes the average person about 15 minutes to walk a mile. Luckily for them, they do not rely on speed to catch their dinners!

This southern African rock python is crawling along the edge of the Cuando River in Botswana, Africa.

Pythons are closely related to boas, another kind of constricting snake. Unlike boas, though, pythons lay eggs. Some kinds of pythons lay the eggs in a nest and then cover them with leaves or dirt. They then wrap themselves around the eggs to keep them safe.

PYTHON HATCHLING

Here a python hatchling is emerging from its egg in the Everglades, in Florida.

Some python moms even work to make sure the eggs are warm enough. They do this by squeezing and relaxing their muscles. The warmth made by these working muscles can raise the temperature of the eggs by a few degrees. When the eggs hatch, the mother python leaves. Most snakes do not care for their eggs or young, at all.

Get Going, Garter Snake!

Garter snakes are a snake many people may be familiar with. Children often find them in the yard or near ponds. They can be from 20 to 30 inches (50–75 cm) long. They tend to have green, yellow, or gray coloring. Most have three yellow or red stripes that run the length of their bodies. Some will flatten their bodies when disturbed to make the pattern stand out more.

This is a red-sided garter snake sunning itself on a rock.

Here you can see how small baby garter snakes can be in comparison to a person's finger.

BIG FACT!

It is not easy being a baby garter snake. More than half the snakes born each year die before they are one year old.

Some snakes are picky about what they eat. Garter snakes will eat anything that comes by that they can catch. They will eat insects, frogs and toads, earthworms, and even tadpoles and bird eggs. They tend to hunt in the early morning, the late afternoon, and the early evening. They choose these times because the Sun is not as strong.

Garter snakes hibernate in winter dens, when temperatures get colder. Thousands of snakes may hibernate in one den. Once spring arrives, the snakes form mating balls outside the den. Female garter snakes give birth to between 15 to 20 babies, though this number can be lower or higher. The babies are usually 7.5 to 9 inches (19–23 cm) long. The babies are born alive and ready to hunt.

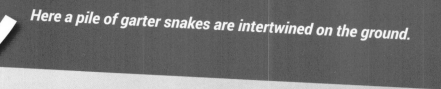
Here a pile of garter snakes are intertwined on the ground.

Garter snakes are an important part of the diet of many animals. Raptors, such as hawks and harriers, eat them. Skunks, raccoons, minks, and house cats catch and eat garter snakes, too. They use their speed to try and get away. They also give off a smelly liquid when grabbed. Unfortunately for them, this does not stop many animals from eating them.

VULTURE

Pythons may eat rodents, birds, lizards, and mammals, such as antelope, pigs, or monkeys. Generally they swallow the prey head first so that the limbs do not get stuck. Pythons do not need to eat every day. In fact, it can take several weeks to **digest** a big meal.

Pythons use their sense of smell to find prey. They also have special heat-sensing pits in their jaws. These pits let the python know if a warm-blooded animal is close by, even if the animal is hiding. Pythons do not chase their prey. They wait for it to pass and then grab it with their teeth before wrapping it up in their coils. Some pythons wait with most of their bodies under water for prey to pass.

Garter Snake Eating

Whether on land or in the water, the end result is the same. Some unlucky animal ends up as lunch!

Garter snakes will eat anything they can catch and kill. They eat slugs, earthworms, leeches, lizards, amphibians, ants, frogs, eggs, toads, and rodents. Garter snakes that live near water will eat the animals that live in the water, such as frogs and tadpoles. Garter snakes will

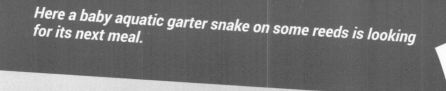

Here a baby aquatic garter snake on some reeds is looking for its next meal.

also sometimes eat eggs. As you can see, these snakes are not picky eaters. They have adapted to eating most anything at anytime it is available, which is how they can live in so many habitats. They chase down prey using their speed, and grab it with their jaws to kill it.

Big OR Small, Does IT Matter?

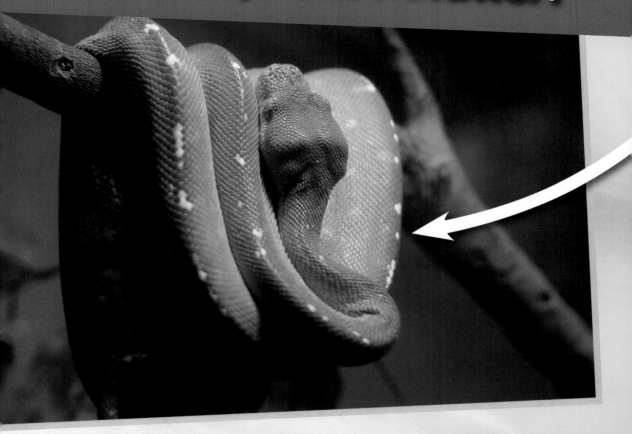

You have learned a lot about garter snakes and pythons. Do you think it is an easier life for the huge python, or for the small garter snake? It is hard to say. Both kinds of snakes have some species that are **endangered**. Both kinds of snakes are often kept as pets and sometimes they are

This tiny garter snake makes a fun and easy pet.

removed from the wild for the pet trade. As with all wild animals, it is better to leave them in their natural habitat. We can learn a lot about our world, by observing the animals that live in it. Pythons and garter snakes are both interesting reptiles, no matter how big they are!

Glossary

adapt (uh-DAPT) To change to fit requirements.

biomes (BY-ohmz) Large communities of plants and animals that are part of one of the worlds major habitats.

carnivores (KAHR-neh-vorz) Animals that eat other animals.

digest (dy-JEST) Breaks down food so that the body can use it.

endangered (in-DAYN-jerd) Describing an animal whose species or group has almost all died out.

invasive species (in-VAY-siv SPEE-sheez) Plants or animals that are brought to a place and drive out the plants and animals that naturally live there.

native (NAY-tiv) Born or grown in a certain place or country.

prey (PRAY) An animal that is hunted by another animal for food.

suffocates (SUH-fuh-kayts) Stops the flow of air to an animal's lungs.

temperature (TEM-pur-cher) How hot or cold something is.

tropical (TRAH-puh-kul) Having to do with the warm parts of Earth that are near the equator.

venom (VEH-num) A poison passed by one animal into another through a bite or a sting.

Index

Websites

Due to the changing nature of Internet links, PowerKids Press has developed an online list of websites related to the subject of this book. This site is updated regularly. Please use this link to access the list: www.powerkids.com/basa/snake/